Handy Vermont Genealogy Handbook

I0450565

By Gary L. Morris

ISBN-13: 978-1507577899

ISBN-10: 1507577893

Table of Contents

Notes

Genealogical Research in Vermont

Vermont has a relatively young and uneventful history, yet there are still many historical and genealogical records and resources available for tracing your family history in the state. Because of the abundance of information held at many different locations, tracking down the records for your ancestor can be an ominous task. Don't worry though, we know just where they are, and we'll show you which records you'll need, while helping you to understand:

- What they are
- Where to find them
- How to use them

These records can be found both online and off, so we'll introduce you to online websites, indexes and databases, as well as brick-and-mortar repositories and other institutions that will help with your research in Vermont. So that you will have a more comprehensive understanding of these records, we have provided a brief history of the "Green Mountain State" to illustrate what type of records may have been generated during specific time periods. That information will assist you in pinpointing times and locations on which to focus the search for your Vermont ancestors and their records.

A Brief History of Vermont

Vermont was first explored by Samuel de Champlain in 1609, and though few settled there over the next 150 years, French, Dutch, English, and Iroquois Indians traversed the area over trails that connected New York and Massachusetts with Montreal. The French briefly set up shop on Isle La Motte in 1666, and there was another short-lived settlement at Chimney Point in 1690. The first permanent settlement Ft. Dummer was built in 1724 near present day Brattleboro.

By 1764 the Governor of New Hampshire, Benning Wentworth, had granted 131 town charters in the territory, claiming that his colony extended as far west as did Massachusetts and Connecticut. In that same year New York claimed Vermont as part of Albany County after the crown established its northeastern boundary at the Connecticut River. Fearing they would lose their land, the New Hampshire land owners formed the Green Mountain Boys, flouting the New York courts and scaring off defenseless settlers from out of the territory.

The Green Mountain Boys helped to capture Ft. Ticonderoga after the outbreak of the Revolutionary War, and the frontiersmen remained a lethal force in the northern theater for the next two years. A Vermont contingent routed German detachments sent by British General Burgoyne toward Bennington after a skirmish at Hubbardton on 16 August 1777, a battle that led to the general's surrender at Saratoga, New York

In 1777 Vermont declared itself an independent republic under the name of "New Connecticut." They drew up a constitution that abolished slavery and providing universal manhood suffrage, while confiscating Tory land and adopting the laws of Connecticut. Most residents were in favor of joining the United States, but the dominant Green Mountain Boys, many of whom had large holdings in the northwest, desired free trade with Canada, even if that meant rejoining the British Empire. The Green Mountain faction was subsequently defeated politically however, and negotiations settled the claims of New York and catapulted Vermont into the Union on March 4, 1791.

Between 1781 and 1810, the population of Vermont exploded from around 30,000 to almost 220,000. The new settlers were spread over the hills in self-sufficient homesteads, and subsequent generations would establish towns with charcoal-fired furnaces, water-powered mills, churches, schools, general stores, craft shops, and printing presses. During the US foreign trade embargo of 1808, northwestern Vermonters were forced to smuggle, and trade with Canada continued through the War of 1812. During the Civil War, Vermont was an avid supporter of the Union cause.

In 1823 the Champlain-Hudson Canal was opened, followed by the early railway lines between 1846 and 1853. Vermont became more vulnerable to western competition, and this period saw many small farms and businesses fail, and many emigrating from the state to greener pastures. Those that remained however gained increasing purchasing power, and they gained a temporary advantage in milk and wool production and cheese making. Light industry expanded and the population was stabilized by the immigration of Irish and French Canadians.

Important Dates in Vermont History

1724 – First permanent settlement established at Ft. Dummer

1764 – New York claims Vermont as part of Albany County. Green Mountain Boys formed

1772 – Scottish colonists found Ryegate and Barnet

1775 – Green Mountain Boys capture Ft. Ticonderoga

1777– Vermont proclaims itself an independent republic

1786– Vermont constitution drafted

1791 – Statehood

1793 – State constitution drafted

Famous Battles Fought in Vermont

Vermont has had a very quiet military history, though the Green Mountain Boys, a band of Vermont frontiersman were largely responsible for the **Capture of Ft. Ticonderoga** during the Revolutionary War.

The battle accounts that exist can be very effective in uncovering the military records of your ancestor. They can tell you what regiments fought in which battles, and often include the names and ranks of many officers and enlisted men.

Capture of Ft. Ticonderoga:
http://www.history.com/topics/capture-of-fort-ticonderoga

Common Vermont Genealogical Issues and Resources to Overcome Them

Boundary Changes: Boundary changes are a common obstacle when researching Vermont ancestors. You could be searching for an ancestor's record in one county when in fact it is stored in a different one due to historical county boundary changes.

The **Atlas of Historical County Boundaries** can help you to overcome that problem. It provides a chronological listing of every boundary change that has occurred in the history of Vermont.

Atlas of Historical County Boundaries: http://publications.newberry.org/ahcbp/documents/VT_Consolidated_Chronology.htm#Consolidated_Chronology

Name Changes: Surname changes, variations, and misspellings can complicate genealogical research. It is important to check all spelling variations. Soundex, a program that indexes names by sound, is a useful first step, but you can't rely on it completely as some name variations result in different Soundex codes. The surnames could be different, but the first name may be different too. You can also find records filed under initials, middle names, and nicknames as well, so you will need to **get creative with surname variations** and spellings in order to cover all the possibilities. For help with surname variations read our instructional article on **How to Use Soundex**.

get creative with surname variations: http://obituarieshelp.org/blog/?p=634

How to Use Soundex: http://obituarieshelp.org/blog/?p=505

Vermont Genealogical Organizations and Archives

Genealogical resources include not only records, but the organizations that house them, or can direct you to them. These institutions include: *Archives, Libraries, Genealogical Societies, Family History Centers, Universities, Churches, and Museums.*

Following are links to their websites, their physical addresses, and a summary of the records you can find there.

<u>Archives and Libraries</u>

Vermont State Archives – Vital records, Naturalizations, Probate records, Military records, Town records, Cemetery records, some Church records

1078 U.S. Rte. 2, Middlesex
Montpelier, Vt. 05633-7701
Telephone: 802-828-3700
Fax: 802-828-3710

Vermont State Archives : http://vermont-archives.org/research/genealogy/

National Archives Northeast Region (Boston) - Federal records of Connecticut, Maine, Massachusetts, New Hampshire, Rhode Island, and Vermont including Census Records, Naturalization Records, Passenger Arrival Lists, Canadian Border Entry Records, Customs Records, Post-Civil War Tax Records, Draft, Military Service, and Pension and Bounty Land Application Files, Chinese Exclusion Act Case Files, Freedmen's Bureau and Records to African American Families, Dawes Commission Final Cards of the Five Civilized Tribes

380 Trapelo Road
Waltham, Massachusetts 02452-6399
Telephone: 781-663-0144 or toll free: 866-406-2379
Fax: 781-663-0154
Website: http://www.archives.gov/boston/

Vermont Department of Libraries – Variety of genealogical and historical resources

109 State Street
Montpelier, VT 05609
Telephone: 802-828-3261

Vermont Department of Libraries: http://libraries.vermont.gov/

Special Collections Bailey/Howe Library - Rare books, periodicals, manuscript collections, historical maps and photographs

University of Vermont
538 Main Street
Burlington, VT 05405-0036
Telephone: 802-656-2138

Special Collections Bailey/Howe Library:
http://library.uvm.edu/sc/

Bennington Museum Research Library – Wealth of historical material, especially regarding the Revolutionary War era

75 Main Street
Bennington, Vermont 05201-2885
Telephone: 802-447-1571

Bennington Museum Research Library:
http://www.benningtonmuseum.org/

Genealogical and Historical Societies

Genealogical and historical societies have access to extensive catalogues of genealogical data. They are also able to offer expert guidance for genealogical researchers. Many members are professional genealogists who are most willing to share their expertise in finding ancestors.

Vermont Historical Society - Family and town histories from around New England, vital records and transcriptions of Vermont cemeteries, genealogical reference books, manuscripts, historical maps and photographs

60 Washington St.
Barre, VT 05641
Tel: (802) 479-8500

Vermont Historical Society - http://vermonthistory.org/research/genealogy/genealogy-research-at-the-vhs

Genealogical Society of Vermont - Marriages in Montpelier, Burlington and Berlin, Vt. 1789-1876, Historical newspapers, family histories and surnames index

P. O. Box 14
Randolph, VT 05060-0014

Genealogical Society of Vermont:
http://www.genealogyvermont.org/

Vermont French-Canadian Genealogical Society - Growing collection of reference books, manuscripts, periodicals and microfiche containing published "repertoires" of church records pertaining to marriages, baptisms and burials

PO Box 65128
Burlington, Vermont 05406-5128
Website: http://vt-fcgs.org/

New England Historic Genealogical Society Library - Vermont Miscellaneous Censuses and Substitutes: 1788-1822, 1840, Vermont Soldiers in World War I, Vermont Vital Records, 1871-2008 plus many county and town level records for Vermont

99 Newbury Street
Boston, MA 02116-3007
Telephone: 617-226-1231

New England Historic Genealogical Society Library:
http://www.americanancestors.org/library/

Vermont Mailing Lists

Mailing lists are internet based facilities that use email to distribute a single message to all who subscribe to it. When information on a particular surname, new records, or any other important genealogy information related to the mailing list topic becomes available, the subscribers are alerted to it. Joining a mailing list is an excellent way to stay up to date on Vermont genealogy research topics. Rootsweb have an extensive listing of **Vermont Mailing Lists** on a variety of topics.

Vermont Mailing Lists:
http://lists.rootsweb.ancestry.com/index/usa/VT/misc.html

Vermont Message Boards

A message board is another internet based facility where people can post questions about a specific genealogy topic and have it answered by other genealogists. If you have questions about a surname, record type, or research topic, you can post your question and other researchers and genealogists will help you with the answer. Be sure to check back regularly, as the answers are not emailed to you. The Vermont Message Boards at **Rootsweb** are completely free to use.

Rootsweb:
http://boards.rootsweb.com/localities.northam.usa.states/mb.ashx

Vermont Newspapers and Periodicals

Many genealogy periodicals and historical newspapers contain reprinted copies of family genealogies, transcripts of family Bible records, information about local records and archives, census indexes, church records, queries, land records, obituaries, court records, cemetery records, and wills. The following sites have historical Vermont newspapers and periodicals that you can search online or on-site.

Genealogical Society of Vermont - Index to Vermont Historical Newspapers

P. O. Box 14
Randolph, VT 05060-0014

Genealogical Society of Vermonto:
http://www.genealogyvermont.org/

GenealogyBank.com – free searchable database of Vermont newspaper archives, 1783-2006

GenealogyBank.com:
http://www.genealogybank.com/gbnk/newspapers/explore/USA/Vermont/

The Online Books Page – links to historical Vermont books and periodicals available for viewing online

The Online Books Page:
http://onlinebooks.library.upenn.edu/webbin/book/browse?type=subject&c=c&key=vermont

Library of Congress Digital Newspaper Directory – free searchable database of historical U.S. newspapers dating from 1690-present

Library of Congress Digital Newspaper Directory:
http://chroniclingamerica.loc.gov/search/titles/

NewspaperArchive.com – largest online database of historical newspapers in the world.

NewspaperArchive.com: http://newspaperarchive.com/

Historical Vermont Maps and Gazetteers

Maps are an integral part of genealogical research. They help us to locate landmarks, towns, cities, parishes, states, provinces, waterways and roads and streets. They also help us to determine when and where boundary changes might have taken place, and give us a visualization of the area we're researching in.

For locating place names, a gazetteer is the best possible resource for any genealogist. Gazetteers are also sometimes called "place name dictionaries", and can help you to locate the area in which you need to conduct research. Below are links to the maps and gazetteers for research in Vermont.

Peabody GNIS Service – Vermonto:
http://peabody.research.yale.edu/cgi-bin/Query.GNIS?ST=Vermont&SU=1

Color Landform Atlas – Vermont:
http://fermi.jhuapl.edu/states/vt_0.html

1985 U.S. Atlas: http://www.livgenmi.com/1895/VT/

Vermont Hometown Locator:
http://vermont.hometownlocator.com/

<u>Vermont City Directories</u>

.

City directories are similar to telephone directories in that they list the residents of a particular area. The difference though is what is important to genealogists, and that is they pre-date telephone directories. You can find an ancestor's information such as their street address, place of employment, occupation, or the name of their spouse. A one-stop-shop for finding city directories in Vermont is the **Vermont Online Historical Directories** which contains a listing of every available online historical directory related to Vermont. Another useful site is **US City Directories** which identifies printed, microfilmed, and online Vermont directories and their repositories.

Vermont Historical Society: Complete listing of every available City Directory in Vermont and the location where they are held. Downloadable Pdf.

Vermont Historical Society:
http://vermonthistory.org/documents/digital/VtCityDirectories.pdf

Vermont Online Historical Directories:
https://sites.google.com/site/onlinedirectorysite/Home/usa/vt

US City Directories: http://www.uscitydirectories.com/sd.htm

Vermont Genealogical Records

<u>Birth, Death, Marriage and Divorce Records</u> – Also known as vital records, birth, death, and marriage certificates are the most basic, yet most important records attached to your ancestor. The reason for their importance is that they not only place your ancestor in a specific place at a definite time, but potentially connect the individual to other relatives. Below is a list of repositories and websites where you can find Vermont vital records.

Vermont Department of Health Birth, Death, and Marriage records after 2007

Vital Records Office
P.O. Box 70
Burlington, VT 05402-0070
Phone: 802-863-7275, or 800-439-5008 (toll free in Vermont)
Email: vitalrecords@state.vt.us

Vital Records Office:
http://healthvermont.gov/research/records/vital_records.aspx

Vermont State Archives – Birth, Marriage and Death records 1760 to 2007

1078 U.S. Rte. 2, Middlesex
Montpelier, Vt. 05633-7701
Telephone: 802-828-3700
Fax: 802-828-3710

Vermont State Archives: http://vermont-archives.org/research/genealogy/

Vermont Historical Society - Microfilmed index to Vermont vital records to 1870

60 Washington St.
Barre, VT 05641
Tel: (802) 479-8500

Vermont Historical Society -
http://vermonthistory.org/research/genealogy/genealogy-research-at-the-vhs

New England Historic Genealogical Society Library - Vermont Vital Records, 1871-2008 plus many county and town level records for Vermont

99 Newbury Street
Boston, MA 02116-3007
Telephone: 617-226-1231

New England Historic Genealogical Society Library:
http://www.americanancestors.org/library/

Family Search has the following indexes that can be searched online for free:

Vermont, Births and Christenings, 1765-1908:
https://familysearch.org/search/collection/1675544

Vermont, Deaths and Burials, 1871-1965:
https://familysearch.org/search/collection/1675549

Vermont, Marriages, 1791-1974:
https://familysearch.org/search/collection/1675550

Vermont, Town Clerk, Vital and Town Records, 1732-2005:
https://familysearch.org/search/collection/1987653

Vermont, Town Records, 1850-2005:
https://familysearch.org/search/collection/1627819

Vermont, Vital Records, 1760-1954:
https://familysearch.org/search/collection/1784223

Vermont, Vital Records, 1760-2003:
https://familysearch.org/search/collection/2075288

Census Records

Census records are among the most important genealogical documents for placing your ancestor in a particular place at a specific time. Like BDM records, they can also lead you to other ancestors, particularly those who were living under the authority of the head of household.

National Archives Northeast Region (Boston) - Federal Census Records 1790-1930

380 Trapelo Road
Waltham, Massachusetts 02452-6399
Telephone: 781-663-0144 or toll free: 866-406-2379
Fax: 781-663-0154

National Archives Northeast Region (Boston):
http://www.archives.gov/boston/

New England Historic Genealogical Society Library - Vermont Miscellaneous Censuses and Substitutes: 1788-1822, 1840

99 Newbury Street
Boston, MA 02116-3007
Telephone: 617-226-1231

New England Historic Genealogical Society Library:
http://www.americanancestors.org/library/

The **Free Census Project** has transcribed many Vermont indexes and new material is added daily

Free Census Project: http://usgwcensus.org/cenfiles/vt.htm

Access Genealogy – Vermont county census records dating from 1790

Access Genealogy:
http://www.accessgenealogy.com/census/vermont-census-records.htm

African American Census Schedules Online – slave schedules, mortality schedules, slave-owners census

African American Census Schedules Online:
http://www.afrigeneas.com/aacensus/ga/

Native Americans in Census Records (US National Archives)

Native Americans in Census Records:
http://www.archives.gov/research/census/native-americans/

Vermont Church Records

Church and synagogue records are a valuable resource, especially for baptisms, marriages, and burials that took place before 1900. You will need to at least have an idea of your ancestor's religious denomination, and in most cases you will have to visit a brick and mortar establishment to view them.

Most church records are kept by the individual church, although in some denominations, records are placed in a regional archive or maintained at the diocesan level. Local Historical Societies are sometimes the repository for the state's older church records. Below are links archives that maintain church records, as well as a few databases that can be viewed online.

The **Family History Library** contains many church records from a variety of denominations on microfilm.

Family History Library:
http://familysearch.org/learn/wiki/en/Family_History_Library

Vermont French-Canadian Genealogical Society - Published "repertoires" of church records pertaining to marriages, baptisms and burials, 1785 to late 1800's

PO Box 65128
Burlington, Vermont 05406-5128

Vermont French-Canadian Genealogical Society: http://vt-fcgs.org/

Central Repositories for Denominational Records

<u>Church of Jesus Christ of Latter-day Saints (Mormons)</u>

Early Mormon Church records for Vermont can be found on film located at the LDS Family History Library in Salt Lake City and can be searched via the **Family History Library Catalog**

Family History Library Catalog:
https://familysearch.org/eng/Library/FHLC/frameset_fhlc.asp

The **Church History Library** has an even broader collection of historical church records than the Family History Library.

Church History Library
15 East North Temple
Salt Lake City, Utah 84150-1600
Phone: (801) 240-2272

Church History Library:
https://history.lds.org/?lang=eng#FlashPluginDetected

<u>Baptist</u>

Bailey-Howe Library
University of Vermont
Burlington, VT 05405-0036
Phone: (802) 656-2020
Fax: (802) 656-4038

Bailey-Howe Library: http://library.uvm.edu/sc/

American Baptist Historical Society
1106 South Goodman Street
Rochester, NY 14620
Phone: (716) 473-1740

American Baptist Historical Society: http://abhsarchives.org/

Congregational

Congregational Library
14 Beacon Street
Boston, MA 02108
Phone: (617) 523-0470
Fax: (617) 523-0470

Congregational Library: http://www.14beacon.org/

Presbyterian

Presbyterian Historical Society
425 Lombard Street
Philadelphia, PA 19147
Telephone: 1-215-627-1852
Fax: 1-215-627-0509

Presbyterian Historical Society http://www.history.pcusa.org/

Methodist

Green Mountain College Library
One College Circle
Poultney, Vt 05764
Phone: (802) 287-8225
Fax: (802) 287-8222 (Attention Library)

Green Mountain College Library: http://www.greenmtn.edu/

Episcopal

Episcopal Diocesan Center
5 Rock Point Road
Burlington, VT 05401-2735
Phone: (802) 863-3431
Fax: (802) 860-1562

Episcopal Diocesan Center: http://diovermont.org/

<u>Roman Catholic</u>

Diocese of Burlington
351 North Avenue
Burlington, VT 05401
Phone: (802) 658-6110
Fax: (802) 658-0436

Diocese of Burlington: http://www.vermontcatholic.org/

Assemblee des Eveques du Quebec
1225 St. Joseph Boulevard East
Montreal, Quebec
Canada H2J 1L7
Phone: (514) 274-4323

Assemblee des Eveques du Quebec: http://www.eveques.qc.ca/

Vermont Military Records

More than 40 million Americans have participated in some kind of war service since America was colonized. The chance of finding your ancestor amongst those records is exceptionally high. Military records can even reveal individuals who never actually served, such as those who registered for the two World Wars but were never called to duty.

Below are a number of links to websites and archives that contain Vermont military records.

Vermont State Archives – Records of the Adjutant and Inspector General from the American Revolution, War of 1812, Vermont Militia, Civil War, Vermont National Guard, Spanish--American War. Collection includes: Medal of Honor recipients, Miscellaneous rolls, Commissions, Hospital records, Bound Manuscript Volumes, Account books, Rosters, and Order books. Also Vermont Militia, Civil War, Vermont National Guard, Spanish--American War, World War I, World War II, Vietnam War records

1078 U.S. Rte. 2, Middlesex
Montpelier, Vt. 05633-7701
Telephone: 802-828-3700
Fax: 802-828-3710

Vermont State Archives: http://vermont-archives.org/research/genealogy/

US Department of Veterans Affairs Nationwide Gravesite Locator – includes information on veterans and their family members buried in veterans and military cemeteries having a government grave marker.

US Department of Veterans Affairs Nationwide Gravesite Locator: http://gravelocator.cem.va.gov/

Family Search has the following indexes which are searchable online for free:

Vermont, Enrolled Militia Records, 1861-1867:
https://familysearch.org/search/collection/1483040

You may also find your ancestor's military records in the following databases:

United States General Index to Pension Files, 1861-1934:
https://familysearch.org/search/collection/1919699

United States Index to Service Records, War with Spain, 1898:
https://familysearch.org/search/collection/1919583

United States Index to Indian Wars Pension Files, 1892-1926 – military pension records of soldiers who fought in the Indian Wars between 1817 and 1898

United States Index to Indian Wars Pension Files, 1892-1926:
https://familysearch.org/search/collection/1979427

United States Registers of Enlistments in the U.S. Army, 1798-1914: https://familysearch.org/search/collection/1880762

United States Mexican War Pension Index, 1887-1926 - index to Mexican War pension files for service between 1846 and 1848:
https://familysearch.org/search/collection/1979390

Civil War Soldiers Service Records - Service records for both Union and Confederate soldiers indexed by soldier's name, rank, and unit.

Civil War Soldier Service Records:
http://go.fold3.com/civilwar_records/

Vermont Cemetery Records

As convenient as it is to search cemetery records online, keep in mind that there are a few disadvantages over visiting a cemetery in person. They are:

- Tombstone information is not always accurately transcribed
- The arrangement of the graves in a cemetery can be crucial as family members are often buried next to each other or in the same grave. This arrangement is not always preserved in the alphabetical indexes that are found online.

With that information in mind, the following websites have databases that can be searched online for Vermont Cemetery records.

Vermont Historical Society – Large collection of Vermont cemetery transcriptions

60 Washington St.
Barre, VT 05641
Tel: (802) 479-8500

Vermont Historical Society:
http://vermonthistory.org/research/genealogy/genealogy-research-at-the-vhs

Vermont Tombstone Transcription Project - death and burial records: http://usgwtombstones.org/vermont/vermont.html

African American Cemeteries Online – African American, slave, and Native American cemetery records

African American Cemeteries Online:
http://africanamericancemeteries.com/ar/

Access Genealogy – database of Vermont cemetery record transcriptions

Access Genealogy:
http://www.accessgenealogy.com/cemetery/vermont-cemetery-records.htm

Find a Grave – over 100 million grave records can be searched on this site. Search can be conducted by name, location, or cemetery name.

Find a Grave: http://www.findagrave.com/

Interment.net - A free online database containing approximately 4 million cemetery records from around the world.

Interment.net: http://www.interment.net/

Billion Graves – as the name implies, you can search a billion records including headstone photos, transcriptions, cemetery records, and grave locations.

Billion Graves:
http://billiongraves.com/pages/search/index.php#cemetery

Vermont Obituaries

Obituaries can reveal a wealth about our ancestor and other relatives. You can search our **Vermont Obituaries Listings** from hundreds of Vermont newspapers online for free.

Vermont Obituaries Listings:
http://obituarieshelp.org/vermont_newspaper_obituaries.html

Vermont Wills and Probate Records

The documents found in a probate packet may include a complete inventory of a person's estate, newspaper entries, witness testimony, a copy of a will, list of debtors and creditors, names of executors or trustees, names of heirs. They can not only tell you about the ancestor you're currently researching, but lead to other ancestors.

Vermont State Archives – Probate recording books and Case files 1778-1996

1078 U.S. Rte. 2, Middlesex
Montpelier, Vt. 05633-7701
Telephone: 802-828-3700
Fax: 802-828-3710

Vermont State Archives: http://vermont-archives.org/research/genealogy/

Family Search has the following indexes that can be searched online for free:

Vermont, Addison County and District Probate Files, 1845-1915 : https://familysearch.org/search/collection/1879935

Vermont, Bennington County, Manchester District Estate Files, 1779-1935: https://familysearch.org/search/collection/1935045

Vermont, Franklin County Probate Records, 1796-1921: https://familysearch.org/search/collection/1921463

Vermont, Orange County, Bradford District Estate Files, 1780-1915: https://familysearch.org/search/collection/1807377

Vermont, Orange County, Randolph District Probate Records, 1790-1935: https://familysearch.org/search/collection/1453983

Vermont, Probate Files, 1800-1921: https://familysearch.org/search/collection/1435692

Vermont, Washington County, Probate Estate Files, 1862-1915:
https://familysearch.org/search/collection/1419704

Vermont, Windham County, Westminster District, Probate Records, 1781-1921:
https://familysearch.org/search/collection/1879202

Vermont Immigration and Naturalization Records

The naturalization process generated many types of records, including petitions, declarations of intention, and oaths of allegiance. These records can provide family historians with information such as a person's birth date and place of birth, immigration year, marital status, spouse information, occupation, witnesses' names and addresses, and more.

If your ancestor lived in or near a large city, or near a city where U.S. courts convened, you may find naturalization records in the **U.S. District Court** before 1906.

U.S. District Court:
http://www.uscourts.gov/FederalCourts/UnderstandingtheFederalCourts/DistrictCourts.aspx

For the rural areas of Vermont, naturalization records may be found with the **County Courts** in each county. Often the records were mixed in with other court proceedings making them difficult to locate. A few counties kept separate records for naturalization. After 1906, all naturalizations were handled in Federal District Courts.

County Courts:
https://www.vermontjudiciary.org/MasterPages/Fav-CourtIndexCalendars.aspx

Vermont State Archives – Naturalization petitions, declarations of intention, and certificates of citizenship from select County and Municipal Courts, as well as petitions and declarations of intention from the United States District Court for the District of Vermont dating from 1811-1972

1078 U.S. Rte. 2, Middlesex
Montpelier, Vt. 05633-7701
Telephone: 802-828-3700
Fax: 802-828-3710

Vermont State Archives: http://vermont-archives.org/research/genealogy/

National Archives Northeast Region (Boston) - Naturalization Records, Passenger Arrival Lists, Canadian Border Entry Records, Customs Records

380 Trapelo Road
Waltham, Massachusetts 02452-6399
Telephone: 781-663-0144 or toll free: 866-406-2379
Fax: 781-663-0154

National Archives Northeast Region (Boston):
http://www.archives.gov/boston/

US National Archives – Immigration records, Naturalization records, Ship's Passenger lists

The National Archives and Records Administration
8601 Adelphi Road
College Park, MD 20740-6001
Tel: 1-866-272-6272; 1-86-NARA-NARAS

US National Archives: http://www.archives.gov/research/guide-fed-records/groups/085.html

Family Search has the following index which can be searched online for free:

Vermont, St. Albans Canadian Border Crossings, 1895-1924:
https://familysearch.org/search/collection/2185163

Vermont Native American Records

National Archives Northeast Region (Boston) - Dawes Commission Final Cards of the Five Civilized Tribes

380 Trapelo Road
Waltham, Massachusetts 02452-6399
Telephone: 781-663-0144 or toll free: 866-406-2379
Fax: 781-663-0154

National Archives Northeast Region (Boston) :
http://www.archives.gov/boston/

Access Genealogy – Vermont Native American census records, tribal histories, and much more

Access Genealogy:
http://www.accessgenealogy.com/native/vermont-indian-tribes.htm

U.S. National Archives - information on American Indians who maintained their ties to Federally-recognized Tribes (1830-1970).

U.S. National Archives: http://www.archives.gov/research/native-americans/

Records of the Bureau of Indian Affairs (BIA):
http://www.archives.gov/research/guide-fed-records/groups/075.html

American Indians Records Repository - records dating from the 1700s including trust, education and other historic Indian Affairs records

American Indian Records Repository
Meritex Enterprises
17501 West 98th Street
Lenexa, KS 66219
Phone: 913-888-0601
Website: http://www.doi.gov/ost/records_mgmt/american-indian-records-repository.cfm

Missing Matriarchs – Resources for Researching Female Vermont Ancestors

Looking for female ancestors requires an adjustment of how we view traditional records sources. A woman's identity was often under that of her husband, and often individual records for them can be difficult to locate. The following resources are effective in locating female ancestors in Vermont where traditional records may not reveal them.

Bibliographies

- *Women in Vermont: A Bibliography,* Marilyn Blackwell (Vermont History 56 (1988) 84-101)
- *Plain and Fancy: Vermont's People and Their Quilts as a Reflection of America,* Richard L. and Donna Bister Cleveland (Quilt Digest, 1991)
- *Collecting Vermont Ancestors,* Alice Eicholz (New Trails, 1986)
- *Green Mountain Girls,* Charles T. Morrissey (Vermont Life, Summer 1973)
- *Those Intriguing Indomitable Vermont Women,* Jean K. Smith (Vermont State Division of the American Association of Women, 1980)

Selected Resources for Vermont Women's History

Bailey-Howe Memorial Library
University of Vermont
Burlington, VT 05405

Shelburne Museum
Shelburne Rd.
Shelburne, VT 05482

Women's Studies Program
Middlebury College
Munroe Hall
Middlebury, VT 06753

Common Vermont Surnames

The following surnames are among the most common in Vermont and are also being currently researched by other genealogists. If you find your surname here, there is a chance that some research has already been performed on your ancestor.

ABBOT, ABBOTT, ABERNATHY, ABORN, ADAMS, ADES, ALDEN, ALDRICH, ALEXANDER, ALLEN, AMBLER, AMERMAN, ANDERSON, ANDREWS, ASKINS, ATWOOD, AUSTIN, AVARANCHES, AYERS, BAKER, BALDWIN, BALL, BARNES, BARRETT, BARROWS, BARRY, BARTON, BATCHELDER, BEARDSLEY, BEASOM, BEECHER, BEMIS, BENNETT, BERRY, BERWICK , BEVILL, BIXBY. BLACK, BLISS, BLODGETT, BLOOD, BOTHWELL, BOYNTON, BROCKETT, BROWN, BUSS, BUTLER, BUTTERFIELD, CAMPBELL, CANDEE, CANTRELL, CHAMBERLAIN, CHANDLER, CHAPMAN, CHASE, CLARK, COBB, COLE, COOK, CRAM, CRON, CROSBY, CUMMINGS, CUTLER, DANIELS, DART, DARTT, DEAN, DEGRAW, DODGE, DOW, DRAPER, DUTTON, DWINEL, DYKE/DIKE, EATON, EGAN, ELLIS, ESTABROOKS, FARNSWORTH, FAUST, FELCH, FISHER, FITCH, FLETCHER, FOLSOM, FOSTER , FOWLER, FRENCH, FULLER, GARY, GEARY, GIBSON, GODDARD,GOULD, GRANT, GREEN, HAINES, HALL, HAMILTON, HANNAFORD, HANSON, HARRINGTON, HARTWELL, HAZELTINE, HAZEN, HENDERSON, HENSON, HILL, HITCHCOCK, HOAR, HODGMAN, HOFF, HOGG , HOLDEN, HOLDREN, HOLLAND, HOLT, HOPKINS, HORACE, HOWLAND, HUSTED, HYLAND, INMAN, IRISH, IVEY, JACKSON, JENKINS,

JENKS, JENNINGS, JERDEE, JOHNSON, JONES, KAPTURE, KEEP, KENDALL, KERBY, KIMBALL, KING, KINNEY, KINSMAN, KNAPP, LANE, LARKEY, LAROCK, LAWRENCE , LEONARD, LEWIS, LOCKWOOD, LUCE, MANCHESTER, MANIFOLD, MARBLE, MARCY, MARKHAM, MARSH, MARSHALL, MARTIN, MASSEY, MAXHAM, MCCANCE, MCDONALD, MCINTOSH, MCNEILL, MELLON, MILLARD, MILLER, MINCHEY, MOHAN , MOORE, MORIN, MORSE, MOSELEY, NARDUZZI, NELSON, NEWTON, NICHOLS, NUTTING, O'REAR, OLBERT, OLCOTT, ORCUTT, OTIS, PAGE, PALMER, PARKER, PARVIN, PATTERSON, PEAKER, PECK, PERKINS, PERRY, PHILLIPS, PIERCE, PIERSON, POOLE, POWERS, PRATT, PRESTON, PROCTOR, PUTNAM, RAYMOND, REDMON, REED, REID, ROBBINS, ROBINSON, ROCKWELL, ROGERS, ROWLAND, RUSSELL, SAID, SANBORN, SAVAGE, SAWYER, SCHNEIDER, SCHREIBER, SCOTT, SEAVER, SEVERANCE, SEYMOUR, SHED, SHEDD, SHEPARD, SIMMONS, SKINNER, SLAIGHT, SMITH, SMITHSON, SNELL, SNIDE, SPAULDING, SPENCER, SPERRY, SPRAGUE , ST SAUVEUR, STEARNS, STEPHENSON, STEVENSON, STEWART, STILES, STOWELL, SYLVESTER, TALBOT, TAYLOR, THOMAS, THOMPSON, TRACY, TUFTS, TUGGLE, TURNER. VANCE. VARNUM, WALDRON, WALKER, WALLIS, WALTON, WARNER, WARREN, WASHBURN, WEBSTER, WELLINGTON, WELLMAN, WESTON, WHEELER, WHITNEY, WILLEY, WILLIAMS, WILLIAMSON, WILSON, WINSLOW, WOOD, WOODRUFF, WRIGHT, YOUNG

Gary L. Morris worked from 2009 to 2014 as a professional researcher for a major player in the genealogy field. After tracing his family lineage back to 1683, he found that genealogy could be an expensive undertaking. As such, has decided to publish these helpful guides to share the valuable free information he has discovered during his career to help others trace their family lineages as inexpensively as possible. An avid genealogist himself, he hopes you will find this guide factual, thorough, helpful, and most of all, effective in helping you to find your family members.